SUPER SHARKS

HAMMERHEAD

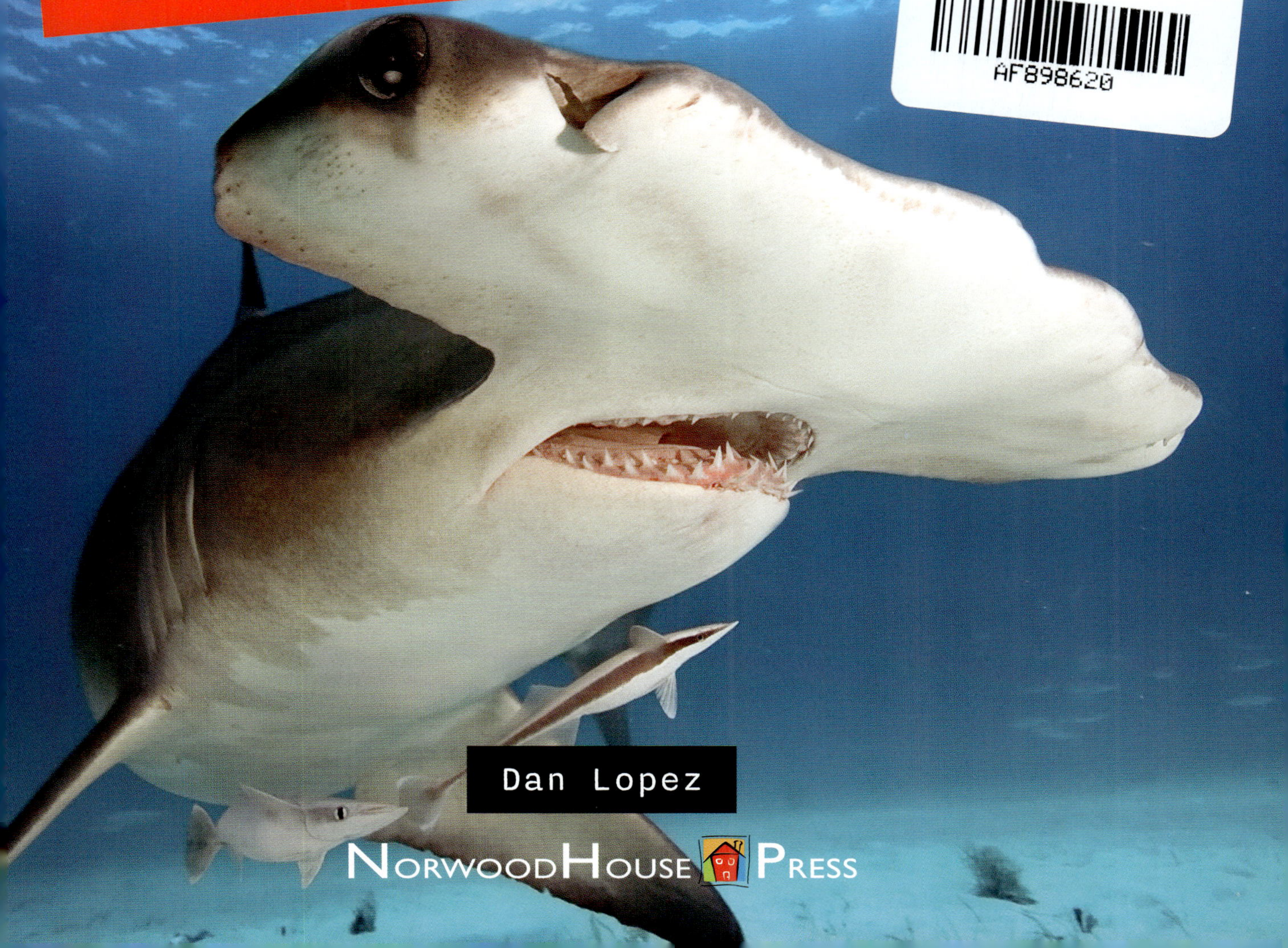

Dan Lopez

NorwoodHouse Press

Cataloging-in-Publication Data

Names: Lopez, Dan.
Title: Hammerhead / Dan Lopez.
Description: Buffalo, NY : Norwood House Press, 2027. | Series: Super sharks | Includes glossary and index.
Identifiers: ISBN 9781978581340 (pbk.) | ISBN 9781978581357 (library bound) | ISBN 9781978581364 (ebook)
Subjects: LCSH: Hammerhead sharks--Juvenile literature.
Classification: LCC QL638.95.S7 L67 2027 | DDC 597.34--dc23

Published in 2027 by
Norwood House Press
2544 Clinton Street
Buffalo, NY 14224

Designer: Rhea Magaro
Editor: Tricia Hoffman

Photo credits: Cover, p. 1 frantisekhojdysz/Shutterstock.com; p. 4 Jsegalexplore/Shutterstock.com; p. 5 wildestanimal/Shutterstock.com; p. 7 Ian Scott/Shutterstock.com; p. 8 Carlos Grillo/Shutterstock.com; p. 9 Matt9122/Shutterstock.com; p. 10 Steve Poole/Shutterstock.com; p. 11 Brad_Beadling/Shutterstock.com; p. 12 Katie Thorpe/Shutterstock.com; p. 15 Alex Vog/Shutterstock.com; p. 16 AaronChenPS2/Shutterstock.com; p. 18 Martin Voeller/Shutterstock.com; p. 19 Drew McArthur/Shutterstock.com; p. 21 Chasity R/Shutterstock.com;

Printed in the United States of America

CPSIA compliance information: Batch #CSNHP27: For further information contact Norwood House Press at 1-800-237-9932.

TABLE OF CONTENTS

What Is Special about Hammerheads?

You could never mistake the hammerhead shark for another animal. Its unusual name matches its unusual looks.

This big fish has a wide, flat, *T*-shaped head. It looks like a double-sided hammer or an ax.

What Do Hammerheads Look Like?

This shark has one eye and one **nostril** on each end of its head. Hammerheads have a great view of what is happening all around. But they have a blind spot right in front. To see straight ahead, they must swing their heads from side to side.

Hammerheads are light gray or brown. Their bellies are white.

A large tail fin helps a hammerhead swim. **Pectoral fins** help with steering. A pair of **dorsal fins** keeps the shark steady. **Gill slits** help the animal breathe.

There are nine **species** of hammerhead sharks. The smallest grows to four feet (1.2 meters) long.

Great hammerheads can be 20 feet (six meters) long! They can weigh 1,000 pounds (450 kilograms).

Where Do Hammerheads Live?

Hammerheads swim in oceans all over the world. They like **tropical** or **temperate** waters. They are found close to land or deep in the ocean.

How Do Hammerheads Hunt?

A hammerhead hunts alone. Its weird head is covered with **sensors** that help it find food. The sensors pick up electrical signals given off by other animals.

A hammerhead looks for crabs, squid, lobsters, and bony fish. Its favorite food is stingrays.

The shark uses its wide head to trap stingrays. It pins them to the ocean floor.

A hammerhead's mouth is on the underside of its head. The mouth is lined with hundreds of **serrated** teeth.

After trapping a stingray, the shark takes big bites. It is not bothered by the stingray's **venomous** barbs.

How Do Hammerheads Reproduce?

Hammerheads do not lay eggs. Mothers give birth to live babies, or pups. Dozens of great hammerhead pups can be born at one time.

GLOSSARY

dorsal fins (DOR-sl finz): flat, thin body parts that stick up from the back of a shark or other marine animal

gill slits (gil slits): openings that let water flow out after it has passed over the gills, which are organs that help an animal breathe by extracting oxygen from water

nostril (NAH-struhl): one of two openings that make up an animal's nose

pectoral fins (PEK-tuh-ruhl finz): fins on both sides of an aquatic animal that act like arms to guide the animal through water

sensors (SEN-surz): body parts that detect and measure changes in the environment and send information to an animal's brain

serrated (SER-ay-ted): notched like the blade of a saw

species (SPEE-sheez): groups of living things that are alike and can reproduce together

temperate (TEM-pur-it): having temperatures that are rarely very high or very low

tropical (TRAH-pi-kuhl): related to parts of Earth that are always hot and rainy

venomous (VEH-nuh-muhs): able to produce and inject a toxic fluid called venom; poisonous

THINKING QUESTIONS

1. Describe the head of a hammerhead shark.
2. How do a hammerhead's fins help it swim?
3. Name something that is about as long as a great hammerhead shark.
4. How does electricity help a hammerhead hunt?
5. What is a hammerhead's favorite food?

Index

About the Author

Dan Lopez lives far from the ocean in Indianapolis, Indiana, with his wife and three kids. He is fascinated by all of Earth's animals, including sharks! He admires their sleekness and speed and thinks more people should appreciate them.